GOLD
OF A
CERTAIN KIND

GOLD
OF A CERTAIN KIND

POEMS

Annemarie Ewing Towner

FITHIAN PRESS, SANTA BARBARA, 1994

DEDICATED TO FRIENDS WHO KEPT THE POEMS ALIVE:

LUE HAWK, EDITH NIELSEN, JUDITH PRONOVOST,
AND JOHN BUTORAC

Some of these poems originally appeared in *Ante, The Christian Science Monitor, Encore, New Poems by American Poets, Rhyme and Reason, Shore Poetry Anthology, Small Pond, Verse in VIEW,* and *Yes.*

Copyright © 1994 Edith D. Nielsen
All rights reserved
Printed in the United States of America

Published by Fithian Press
A division of Daniel & Daniel, Publishers, Inc.
Post Office Box 1525
Santa Barbara, CA 93102

Design by Eric Larson

LIBRARY OF CONGRESS CATALOGING-IN-PUBLICATION DATA
    Towner, Annemarie Ewing, 1905–1981.
        Gold of a certain kind : poems / Annemarie Ewing Towner.
            p.   cm.
        ISBN 1-56474-081-1
        I. Title.
    PS 3570.O914G65   1994
    811'.54—dc20   93-37525
                                                            CIP

Annemarie Towner was a teacher, a classical pianist who liked to start every morning by playing a Bach prelude ("it clears the mind," she said), a jazz enthusiast, and a lover of popular music who knew the words to hundreds of songs from Stephen Foster to Cole Porter to Paul Simon. (And she danced a wicked soft shoe.) But always, and above all, she was a poet. She had the poet's passion for the right word, the right sound, the right rhythm. She was willing to tackle some of the most difficult poetic forms, the Welsh meters, because she relished the serendipitous insights and revelations of emotions that strict forms can bring to a writer. But even if we don't consciously appreciate the forms, we appreciate what the forms contain: her humane meditations on relationships, on the solitary sojourner in the natural world, and on the quest for the truth of the moment, whether the seeker is Pine Top Smith with his boogie-woogie piano, William Blake, or her own father playing his violin in a vaudeville theater. These poems are gifts. We can all be grateful that she left them for us.

NORMA ALMQUIST, EDITOR

CONTENTS

I. SOME OF THE GIRLS

LADY OF THE WILD THINGS

Who among you
if your child wanted a dog
would give her a wolf?
I do so...

It is still small,
beautiful as a toy collie,
will go with you to dog-training school,
sit, heel, beg prettily, take the leash,
roll over and play dead.

Nevertheless, it is a wolf
and begins to remember
in artery and bone
prowling and howling the moon
eyes oblique   ears erect
Its padded feet begin to throb
nights
to an ancient earth contact
a round-and-round on hard ground
nose sniffing   wind ruffing the tail
muffled drumbeat feet thudding
    wild   wild   wild

(Did you want your child to heel,
beg prettily, trot leashed, play dead?)

Cherish my wolf...

LOVER, TELL ME...

Lover, tell me of your mother,
Ere I love thee,
Ere I love thee;
Lover, ere I trust me to thee,
Tell me of your mother.

Was she saintly like Madonna,
Hard to win,
Thought it sin
If she let the living in?
Was she like Madonna?

Or was she Madame your Mother,
Headed she
The family?
Lover, did you bend the knee
To Madame your Mother?

Tell me, did she love your father,
Let him know it—
Did he know it?
Lover, did your mother show it
That she loved your father?

Or, love, did she hate your father,
Scornful she,
Secretly,
Of his man meat. If this be,
How shall you be father?

And her children—did she love you,
Sister, brother,
Sister, brother,
Did you know among each other
That your mother loved you?

How shall I know, save through the woman
Who begot you,
Loved or fought you,
Shaped or twisted, tamed or taught you,
If you can love woman?

So tell me, lover, of your mother,
Ere I love thee,
Ere I love thee,
Lover, ere I trust me to thee,
Tell me of your mother.

BALLAD, AMERICAN MYTHIC

Mother mine, mother mine, what do you see?
What do you see when you look at me?
    I see my ambitions all trampled and torn
    By a daughter who won't be a lady born.

Mother mine, Mother mine, were I a son,
What would you see if I were a son?
    I'd see the tempter, the masculine hex,
    The inescapable threat of sex.

Mother mine, Mother, is that why you stare
At the poor man in greasy overalls there?
    Man? I see Misery, Poverty's clerk,
    Coming home dirty each night from work.

Mother mine, Mother, be yet more clear:
Describe more exactly this good woman here.
    Woman? What woman? I see a nice house,
    Obedient children, conformable spouse;
    God Bless Our Security clearly their motto;
    They behave as the nice woman thinks that they ought to.

Mother mine, dam us—but don't think to sire us
As well, with this virus a-lodge in your iris.
Neither moteless nor beamless, but sightless the eye
That sees things and not people. Dear Mother, goodbye…

SCOTCH-IRISH IS A DIFFICULT THING TO BE

My grandmother told me the legend long ago
Of the Irish-born but Scotch-bred Rosie O'—
O'Donal it was. She was wanderer Donal's daughter,
Daft minstrel Donal who sang so sweet by the water
That plunges down Ben Lomond in steel-bright foam
That he summoned a faery he had known back home.
He bowed. Harp-heavy, he slipped and fell from the brim
To the pool below, which silenced the harp—and him.
'Twas a swan song of fecklessness. (He could not swim.)

His orphan waxed tall and fair and grave of mien.
The lonely lanes that lead to Loch Katrine
Had never looked on bonnier alien lass.
Heather and gorse in every mountain pass
Bloomed but to beg her comeliness to sing
As befit her birth. Rosie O' did no such thing;
Her habit of sober songlessness deemed wise.
Had not daft Donal's singing caused his demise?
The village had told her so. (They told her lies.)

For forty years she labored to refute
Her father's fatal gift by remaining mute.
'Tis true she labored usefully. She fell
Upon all tedious tasks and did them well.
The sick she tended and the young she taught.
In trouble she was Rosie-on-the-spot.
Till into her bones there slipped a weariness
And over her eyes a veil of vacantness.
"What ails me? death?" she whispered. (They said, "Yes.")

Then up rose Rosie O' at her own wake.
"And did I fear to sing for safety's sake?"
She bayed at the village. "Not sing at all for fear
I'd die of it? Whisht, I've *been* dead these forty year!"
So saying, into the moonbright night she leapt,
Singing like one demented. The village crept
Away to watch her over the waterfall ride,
Daft as Donal, her winding sheet astride.
"'Twas the songlessness near did me in!" she cried.
Thereafter she never stopped singing. (And never died.)

MOTHER'S DAY

Little-boy time passes
into man-time. How does
the shift from puppy to grown-up
come about? Best *via* myth, vow,
rite, dream. In this dream we *goys*,
both Scots, attend the Bar Mitzvah.

The right rain has brought me
and my son to see
the Jewish boy-initiate,
robed in pubescence, falter
over his passage of Scripture.
His mother prompts her candidate

for manhood. *Mazeltov!* Now we
mothers greet each other, knowing
what's new here, what revival
has restored us to the Temple,
maternal Israeli and Gael:
People of the Book. Female.

The Word becomes flesh; the sky
bursts open with tidings of great joy.
The hair at the back of our neck
bristles; the Fire scorches our cheek.
Oy, Adonai…? Lo, our Father…?
Not necessarily.

Ah, Inanna…Ishtar…
Hothar   Rhea   Demeter
(Who, in the Beginning, were)
Shalom and Welcome, Life-Giver,
multi-titled Earth-Mother,
Here, thank Goddess, You are once more!

NAMING

"Whatsoever Adam called
every living creature
that was the name thereof..."

At fifteen, I learned about naming
unknown to Adam
from my piano teacher,
widely known in Pittsburgh musical circles
as Camille Maher.

When I reached the Adagio
of the Grieg Concerto, she,
late in life for a woman,
married my father's fiddle teacher, whose name
was Theodore Rentz.

Mr. and Mrs. Rentz: a happy union—
concerted in Bach and Brahms
and Beethoven sonatas—
during which he habitually called her
"my wife, Miss Maher..."

WOMAN'S SONG

Make haste! to the treadle   the needle
    The cradle   the potting shed
       not enough hours in the day
       between breakfast and bed...

        the young woman said

Are the geese plucked?
    peas plucked?   corn shucked?
Don't dare dawdle!
          Is the fortune made?
      account book tidied?   reserves readied?
      See how the years rocket ahead...

        the young woman said

Let me help you   trundle you placid
    out to the beachhead
    all this hullabalooing rockabyed
Let me tortoise you forward
    to where you came from
I'm in no hurry   I have so little time...

        the old woman said

TANTE GUITE TURNS 71

The water she swims in is shallower
Says it buoys her up better
The miles she walks are fewer
Pace slower   Discoveries simpler:
"Have those wild asters
been growing all these years
beside that box elder?"

She speaks more rarely:
Woodruff and woodlark most nearly
Share the quality
Of her May-wine words, their bird-throat clarity

She has sleepless nights oftener
Likes, she says, an extra hour
To be aware in.   Says, around four,
It sometimes occurs to her
That she burns with a quieter fire

READY OR NOT

I was much older when I was young,
Knew a lot more.
Show me a book, I could spout what was wrong
Hour after hour.
I was quite sure—
And could prove it with quotes from Freud and Jung—
Why a marriage went sour.

All those years back when I was older,
Could plot a course,
Tell how much coin—to the nearest guilder—
Bought the winning horse.
I was fierce
In defense of the right, a never-yielder,
Job in reverse.

I have attained my nonage now.
My favorite game:
Scanning this seed until I spy
Chrysanthemum
In so small room
Contained, hidden I don't know how...
Any number can play.˙

PORTRAIT

> *"My happiness wears a sad face..."*
> —Iris Murdoch

My happiness wears so sad a face
I turn away my eyes.
Harlequin countenances I notice
but her steadfast gaze
(my happiness wears a face so sad
and demanding) I avoid.

Lord Eat, Lady Drink, Mistress Merry—well met,
on-the-way-to-death revelers!
My happiness sits there perfectly quiet,
absorbed in forlorn raptures,
her Easter tears so Magdalen
you can hardly tell them from rain.

You can hardly tell her *miserere*
from *jubilate*, so sure
her ground bass. Let scatter airy
cadenzas of fluttering laughter
while I embrace, incredulous,
my fugue-firm happiness,

while I re-kindle my eyes from her eyes
luminous as a child's
soberly watching an ant dispose
of its bread-crumb burden. Wilds
of desert still unrosed summon
me to her solemn welcome.

BROTHERS

Yesterday I discovered that my spouse
has a pagan brother
who chooses to live in remote heathen countries
known by names most of us can not pronounce.
My husband rather
envies (but scoffs at) his brother's acceptance

of incidents beyond his credence
in places where anyone's eight-stringed cither,
held up to the wind, makes music; where market place faucets
give anyone water, wine, or milk on request;
where people, whether
working or playing, seem to be dancing.

My brother-in-law also speaks of goddesses
who are much blither
than any deities permitted us,
their wisdom so ancient it has grown joyous,
who never bother
with power, find ludicrous

the rant and bluster of whiphand bosses,
machos of either
this world or the next. The question arises:
have I been living in the wrong place
with the wrong brother?
Time to make a cannier choice.

LINES TO A PROBABLY UNLISTENING GRANDDAUGHTER

"Gather ye rosebuds while ye may…"
Hop into bed, that is to say
Before you're faded, going gray,
And no young blood will bid you play
Merrily with him in the hay.
"Cueillez, cueillez, vostre jeunesse…"
Even in French the thought is less
Seductive than the poetry.
Admire the metaphor completely,
But murmur to yourself discreetly,
"Surely nobody supposes
My life's as fragile as the rose's!"

The theme of instant love, please note,
Is one on which male poets dote.
It's not so rife where women are;
They know what Herrick and Ronsard
Were getting at. They speculate
That now-or-never is not the threat
It was. They see it more as bait
Than banquet; they even metaphor thus:
The gander often finds the sauce
Spicier than does the goose.

Granddaughter, the act of love's not equal,
With or without reproductive sequel.
Sex is not basically mathematic
Nor physical congress democratic.
One body holds an inner room,
Deeper even than the womb,
As vulnerable to psychic as
To physical wound. Granddaughter, pause
A moment when you're urged to bride you
Briefly, to take this man inside you.
One into one can come out zero,
Minus heroine, minus hero.
Leave equations to algebra classes.
Learn to value your differentnesses.

THE AUSTRALIAN TURNS UP IN A DREAM

From such a distance away
And such a long time ago
He appears now as if he

Had just laid down his violin
After the day's practice routine
In that student pension

In Paris. My New York living room
Accepts his gentle aplomb.
He is perfectly at home.

"There is no feeling better
Than this of being together,
Little one," he says. (Whatever

He said touched the harmonic
Always, the overtonic
Upper pitches of magic,

Of orderly revelation.)
"But I can reveal only
What I first told you, little one."

I settle down to listen.
"Together is often alone,"
He says, "like the moon, like the sun."

DRUMMER

What you hear is a harp, they told her,
A virginal, lyre, or dulcimer.

I hear a drum, she said.

Drums beat in jungles, on fields of battle,
At state parades or funerals.

It's not that kind of drum, she said.

Hang your head. There's but one kind of rhythm.
We will drum you out of the regiment.

Paradiddle to you, she whispered.

But she hung her head while her inner ear
Stayed ever alert. When she was sure,

I hear one hand drumming, she said.

As if summoned, he came into focus.
The one-handed drummer smiled and spoke:

Give me your hand and lift up your head.

Even their trial team-handed drumbeat
Sounded more like promise than threat.

This is more like it, she said,

Double-drumming away. They called after her,
Where do you think you're going, traitor?

You'll know when you hear us, she said.

LADY REVOLUTIONARY

I like thinking about Miss Dickenson
stitching together her packets
of poems, tidy stacks
of prim note paper, four to six
sheets each, tucking them neatly
away in a drawer
of her cherrywood bureau

In her placid bedroom overlooking
tree-cool Main Street in Amherst, Mass.,
this lady revolutionary stockpiled
her explosives, packed with delicate
precision language mechanisms,
timed to go off later in our dud ears,
aimed at everlastingness
whither she had, by target time, escaped.

SOMETHING NEW IN DEITIES

The statue of the Lady turns its head
in a slow semicircle.
Her smile is seraphical
but also wryly amused.
Then the statue speaks
and everyone listens, awed as well as delighted.

Certain devices of divinity are present
in this dream: voice
from unlikely place—burning bush
of Moses, for instance;
nod from sacred Greek or Roman
statue. Such goings-on, miraculous and masculine,

were, in old holy books, devoutly noted:
when the statue of the god
Zeus or Apollo moved,
when the Voice spake,
Deity had happened
and had better be believed. This lady

is not Zeus nor Apollo nor Moses
in disguise.
Nevertheless
when a dream like this
happens, it is obvious
that something new in Deities is taking place.

II. WELSH METERS

Some of the Welsh poetic forms date from the sixth century A.D. Welsh poets studied their art for years before they could call themselves professionals. There was even a guild of bards, the Eistedfodd, which convened yearly and regulated the affairs of the profession, such as the establishment of metrical rules and the issue of licenses to those who had completed their apprenticeship. No free verse there.

Here are some of the meters used in this collection:

ENGLYN   Thirty syllables, with the main rhyme first occurring on the seventh, eighth, or ninth syllables and then on the 16th, 23rd, and 30th.

RHUPYNT   A twelve-syllable line of three sections, each having four syllables, the first section rhyming with the second, the 12th syllable bearing the main rhyme, and a consonantal correspondence woven around the main stresses of the second and third sections.

CYWYDD   Rhyming couplets (aa,bb), each line having seven syllables with the accentuation of the rhyming endings uneven, i.e., penultimate in one and final in the other.

PRAIRIE PEOPLE *(rhupynt)*

"For the wind passeth over it, and it is gone..."
—Psalms 103:6

Always the wind
Scouring the land
Clean as a rind
Sweeping all chaff
From ripened wheat
The prairie lies flat
Under his swift
Winnowing staff.

We prairie-born
Need never learn
Who howls in the barn
Need not inquire
Who's making moan
In the weather vane.
We have always known
The wind is there.

We prairie-bred
Are not dismayed
However loud
The wind may flail
However near
He passes over.
Why should we fear?
We know him well.

MOTHER OF NECESSITY *(combined englyn unodl union and englyn unodl crwca)*

The mother of Invention we can name:
Old Dame Necessity,
Alias Lady Up-a-Tree,
Madame Impasse, Frau What-Now,

Whose son made the wheel; we go farther faster,
No need to carry
Even the burden of ourselves.
Why was he in such a hurry?

He made a bridge called Faith across Despair
Where many safely pass,
Grateful, singing his praises.
What brought him to the abyss?

Observe also Invention's sister:
Her marriage is a disaster.
See her Inventing ways to bolster a life
Of wifelessness with a monster

Of a husband. She, in time,
May triumph over her doom.
But what made her marry him in the first place?
Trace the answer closer home…

What gets us into each spot
Out of which we can not get
Without those feats of ingenuity
Mother Necessity taught us?

Go ask the name of her who silent sits
And knits beside the chimney.
Grandam of Invention, she,
Mother of Necessity.

POET: MIDWEST   *(englyn penfyr)*

For I.L.S.

She grew up like a Kansas sunflower,
Pioneer-sturdy, golden
And straight in the wind-tossed grain.

Childhood nights her father read Scott aloud,
Shakespeare also, by kitchen lamplight:
Such nurture made her poet.

Tasting words as honey slow-sipped, her hungry
Tongue savored their sweetnesses.
She fancied poets as bees

Till she was eighty. Friends had fled the field
Her brood had been harvested.
Husband had died. She waited.

When she was lonely, she wrote sestinas.
Tackling this tough verse pattern
Leaves you no time for self-pity.

ELEGY FOR IDA LOWRY SINCLAIR *(englyn milwr)*

Composed in old Welsh meters she liked upon words read at her funeral

> *"...his days are as grass..."*
> —*Psalms 103:15*

The grass that made up her days
Was kin to sparrow (See Benet's
Poem which she memorized)

Sparrows don't require very
High flying, can be merry
Anywhere, also wary,

The way skeptics often are,
And brave, though their valor
Threatens no one with "Beware!"

And may be observed only
By an eye as sharp as their own.
Grass could be sparrow's twin!

Identical the spirit
To survive, grin and bear it,
To be earth's gay green cocked hat

Things keep getting knocked into,
Yanked out again somehow
In brief days of grass and sparrow.

Step on grass, it springs back hale,
Thumbs its nose at your heel,
Covers war's deepest shell hole.

SCHOOL TEACHER'S FRIDAY NIGHT *(englyn penfyr)*

I shall die now simply of weariness,
slow-pressed to Finis where here
I lie, student themes my bier,
red pencil in hand supine and inert,
unhurt, just honed to a fine
thin line, graded D minus.

D for Deceased—from a score of classes,
of masses of kids a-roar
all day; PTA at four;
lesson planning for children who can't learn
or—what's worse—who don't care to;
my after-school club, and I'm through.

Strew text books grimed and torn at my feet and head;
tread softly and look forlorn.
I'll rise up Monday morning.

FOR R.L.S. *(cyhydedd hir)*

"...tongue in cheek and hand on heart...a true Stevenson gesture..."
—*Margaret Mackay, in* The Violent Friend: The Story of Mrs.
  Robert Louis Stevenson

Tongue in cheek and hand
On heart, one may stand
Armed, against the wound
Life's bound to give.
Knife point there will be:
At throat? at artery?
Keep the smile leery,
The heart alive.

There was a Scotsman
Of this doughty clan.
He faced with a grin
Old "Bluidy Jack":
Wrote hard, arm in sling
To save his bad lung.
How's that for a tongue
In bloody cheek?

Pursued his bonny
Girl to Monterey;
Shipped steerage, for he
Was poor as dirt.
Rode like immigrant
Across this broad land.
How's that for a hand
On loving heart?

Life's full of plenty
You can not prevent,
Much grief you don't want:
Tongue in cheek saves,
Pertly parries blows
As long as it knows
The sturdy heart as
Sturdily loves.

BIBLIOGRAPHICAL NOTE *(awdl gywydd and toddaid)*

When his angels told Blake to write, he did.
He said his words flew sprightly
from the page until he had
a roomful of bird words, lightly
perching with alphabet feet on the mantel.

His room then hummed with feathery rhymings
from chair back to bed canopy:
stanzas soared on inky wings,
pen-point beaks piped prosody.
Such an aviary could only be Blake's.

He always rose from his chair, sweetly content,
announcing his work completed,
indeed, already in print
for Angel Press. He won't want
the manuscript. Why not burn it?
Fortunately, his wife would not let him.

ROLFE HUMPHRIES: AMERICAN BARD *(d. 1969)*

Some ancient birthmark
Cymric-Druid dark
At last came full arc
To make him bard.
His ear became quick
To all the magic
Music Dafydd struck
From every word.

In a foreign tongue
He shaped shaft and wing
Of *englyn*, chain-rhyming,
And *cynghanedd.*
Great became his skill.
Younger poets will
Surely be thankful,
Follow his path.

Had he been Arverni-
Born, he'd have been high
Bard, throat never dry,
At the King's table,
Equally proud
To sing, love, drink mead,
Lead the raid—should deed
And steed be noble.

Bard blood has run dry.
No bard stands as high
As a physicist's eye
In our grim time
Of the one-track mind,
Electronic sound.
Bard-proud he remained.
He held the dream.

Craft chaos may well
Fill verse with offal;
He held out for skill,
Praise, and discipline.
He taught the young to rhyme,
Loved a good ballgame,
Called cravenness crime,
Apathy sin,

Found today's monarch
In thoroughbred: *Dark
Star*, say, to win. Mark
And training tell.
He would like best
This hail for his last:
Weather clear, track fast…
Champion, farewell!

*Rolfe Humphries, poet, professor, translator of Welsh bards and Latin
poets, was the leading American authority on Welsh meters.
Annemarie Towner wrote her Master's Thesis on his use of Welsh
meters and later studied under him in his poetry workshops.*

JOHN KEATS TAKES HIS LEAVE *(awdl gywydd)*

I would have preferred to go
From you with a show of grace,
Of disarming charm, gravely
Waving a kerchief of lace.

Perhaps with a word or two
On a subdued, rueful note,
Wryly witty, faintly fey,
That someone later might quote.

But I could never acquire
The foxfire retort, the art
Of the polished gesture to mask
The casket in the heart.

Sodden with fever, as death
Chokes the breath in the throat, so
I must go, now as always
Awkward at making a bow.

*"I always made an awkward bow": last sentence of Keats' last letter,
30 November 1820.*

III. JAZZ POEMS

PINE TOP SMITH *(d. 1928)*

Here he played...
   With a boom-a-lang-a-boogie
   And a boom-a-lang-a-woogie
   With a rub-a-dub-dub
   A pi-ya-na for a tub
  Whatcha *call* that, man? What, man? *That*, man!
  Noise like someone rollin' bowlin' balls in a vat
  Noise like flock o' locomotives loose on a grade
  Call that music, man? Mr. Pine Top spat
  On his hands like he was gonna pound them ivories
   with a spade.
  Call it sumpin' in between a stampede and a shout
  Call it sumpin' lets a glory in the blood git out
  Call it boogie woogie. Mr. Pine Top calls it that.

Here he stayed...
  In Chicago...Chicago, that toddlin' town
  On State Street, ev'ry late street, they gathered aroun'
  And they marveled how he pounded that pi-ya-na outa plumb
  Mr. Pine Top lammed them keys like a drum, like a drum.
  They took him to a studio and spun a platter flat:
  Pine Top's Boogie Woogie. Mr. Pine Top called it that.
  "Come back next week." The record people wanted more
  Of that glory in the blood. But there wasn't no more.

Here he laid...
  It was noon at the studio. Recording time was gone.
  "Like I told you, those jigs can't be depended on."
  His wife came in. "They was an accident," she said.
  "He got hisself cut up. He can't come. He dead."

  Lay him low lay him out
  In between a stampede and a shout
  And a glory in the blood that's gotta git out.
  Bury him deep in the ground
  Old pi-ya-na keyboard on his mound
  And ev'ry night at twelve o'clock all glory bustin' loose
  Like a flock o' locomotives banged together in a noose
  Ev'ry skeleton in scarlet skirt or derby hat
  Stompin' to his boogie woogie. Mr. Pine Top called it that.

ROYAL FAMILY, U.S.A.

I. THE KING

> *For God's sake, let us sit upon the ground*
> *And tell sad stories of the death of kings...*
> *—King Richard II, Act III, scene ii*

Joe Oliver.   Papa Joe.   King Oliver.
Title by right of conquest. First and best
Of New Orleans trumpet men. Young Louis Armstrong
Was proud to carry Papa Joe's horn in parades
So all the winded King had to do was walk
And sweat and miss the piles of horse manure.
Besides parades, played the honky-tonks
In Storyville: Pete Lala's. Funky Butt Hall.
Was so good he made it to Chicago.
Played the Plantation. Presently sent for Louis.
(He'd given the kid his first real horn, a York.)

Was royalty also by right of temperament.
Dispensed largesse of music. *Noblesse oblige*:
The obligation of his nobility
Was to be so generous of audience
That he would keep on playing long past the time
His teeth went numb, pressed too long against the mouthpiece;
His lips, held too long in embouchure, split. And bled.
(A horn man's life hangs on his lips and teeth.)
But His Royal Highness never counted the choruses.
In *Dippermouth Blues*, say, he went the whole gutbucket.
"Play that thing!" His Majesty's sole command.
(Your genuine monarch is no bookkeeper;
He doesn't dribble out choruses for profit,
Nor bank exuberance to buy self-preservation.)
His Majesty was not sensibly frugal with glory.

And so the grief began. Used up when he hit New York.
Lip shot. Teeth loosened with pyorrhea.
(A horn man's life hangs on his lips and teeth.)
Drifted back South. Small bands with smaller musicians.
Vegetable stand outside Savannah, Georgia.
Janitor's job cleaning up a local bar.
And one last one-night stand, backstage with Louis.
One happy night among his loyal subjects:
Old Lear in high button shoes and a box-back coat;
Old Richard Second, still the King of his griefs.
After that, he died. A heart attack?
Depends entirely what you mean by heart.
"Couldn't go no further with grief," Louis said.

II. THE DUKE: A PORTRAIT *(c. 1940)*

The Duke makes his aristocratic entrance…

    (Ducal coronet a Stetson hat
creamy *café au lait* in color, nobly wide of brim,
doublet a soft-as-silky flannel shirt
open at the throat, also *café au lait,*
likewise his camelhair cape
draped carelessly from his titled shoulders.
They say he puts a fortune on his back. What Duke does not?

        He has this night presided,
        he has, indeed, provided
        a musical entertainment
        a masque   a revelry
        sometimes called a University
        Spring Prom

    (He has his own orchestra, of course;
no princely court should ever be without one:
Beethoven had Lichnowsky's; Haydn, Esterhazy's.
Poor Mozart, having none,
starved and died too soon)

It's time for midnight supper in the banquet hall…

        Before his Grace condescends to sup
        he jots down a musical idea or two:
        something for tomorrow's entertainment?
        some courtly folderol or fiddledeedee?
            Apparently
        for His Grace writes music lightly, swiftly, fluently,
        the way other people write letters.
        Something new for horns in "Echoes of Harlem"?
        New bridge between sections of "Black and Tan Fantasy"?
        He stuffs the score in his pocket carelessly.
        Lots more where that came from.

(Lots more will include "In the Beginning God",
"David Danced before the Lord with all his Might":
jazz bursting with worship, performed in churches,
also a Pulitzer award not given
and a seventieth birthday party at the White House)

But now his musicians join him at supper...

His sort of page boy, jester, madcap drummer
has taken over the cooking (even the chef laughs!)
true, only Kings permit such impudent fellows,
but this one followed this Duke from their native
province
and none can resist the gaiety or the rhythm
of Sonny of Greer

So let the banquet begin...

The Duke of Ellington now lowers his person
to the broken stool
in front of the grimy counter
under the fly-specked lights
revealing the dirty floor
of the only place in town where he will be served:
the dingy railroad station restaurant
in Urbana, Illinois

III. THE COUNT *(d. 1984)*

The Count sits, gravely happy
at his black and white keyboard
grinning with his lips but somber about the eyes.
His phallic fingers quest among the keys.
They tinkle merrily, merrily in the treble
and dire away   DOOM   DOOM   DOOM:
the doom's in the bass.

(O it's gather ye gather ye roses in the treble
And *Kyrie Eleison* in the bass)

His musicians cradle in arms,
crooning or chuckling into
twisted brass and hollowed wood
caressing or whaling the daylights out of
hoops of tautened hide;
while he himself hovers tenderly, fatherly,
over ivory and ebony in a harp-shaped coffin,
a grin on his face as wide as the eighty-eight,
and sorrow in his eyes.

(Yes, it's gather ye gather ye roses in the treble,
And *Christe Eleison* in the doom doom bass)

There's no place he'd rather be—
That's clear as a new-born tear—
Than here in this studio gaunt as any cathedral
and empty of rosiness as any tomb,
tinkling and dooming his way through "How Long Blues"
grinning and questing his way through "One O'Clock Jump"

(with its gather ye gather ye roses in the treble
And *Kyrie Eleison* in the bass)

Edward, Count Basie, at his piano sits
Squaring the ancient circle of opposites
His treble grin makes merry, nor denies
The doomsday sadness bass-grieving in his eyes.

DJANGO REINHARDT *(d. 1953)*

Django was a gypsy.
He had but fingers three
with which to play on his guitar.
But did he suffer? No, not he,
though he was genuine Romany
and you know how gypsies are:

born to the purple vibrato,
the lachrymose violin bow;
jazz musicians they are not,
but troubadours of amorous woe.
So how did Gypsy Django know
how to play *le vrai jazz hot?*

He lived, by choice, like a gypsy
with his gypsy family
in a wagon, and where he felt like staying,
he stayed: sometimes Nice, Paris usually,
maybe parked beyond the *Porte de Clichy,*
and he played when he felt like playing.

Employment he found a nuisance,
but sometimes he gave it a chance,
worked in a Montmartre hole-in-the-wall,
or with the Quintette of the Hot Club of France.
And sometimes he showed up in ragged pants,
and sometimes not at all.

Django Reinhardt's triad
of fingers, good or bad,
were plenty to catch the music he caught,
since what goes into *le vrai jazz hot*
comes out of fingers you haven't got,
or didn't know you had.

BIX BEIDERBECKE *(d. 1931)*

Beiderbecke Beiderbecke trumpet man
Play me a tune as quick as you can
Tongue it and valve it and try it in C
And put it on wax for Old Age and me.

    Out of the Corn Belt U.S.A.
    Out of Davenport I   A
    Comes this mid-Western Gabriel
    This Orpheus all the way home from Hell
    Skinny as a scarecrow stick-out ears
    Able to blow anything he hears
    Tone like well water tart and pure
    Drips from his natural embouchure
    Never owned a whole tux in his life
    Never a house or a bond or a wife
    College kids tagged along after this thin
    Big-eared Pied Piper of Hamelin.

    Got him a job at a Princeton frat
    Had a bad cold but who cares about that
    There's music to make that's all a man needs
    Caught pneumonia on that date
    Died at the age of twenty-eight
    Open the mountain and let him in
    His own Pied Piper of Hamelin.

When I am seventy seventy-five
Tottering doddering hardly alive
Bent in the back bent in the knee
Arteries hardening audibly
Before you write my epitaph
Play me a tune on the phonograph
Wa Da Da   Ostrich Walk   Jazz Band Ball
Any old Beiderbecke tune at all
And I will rise up from my rockin' chair
Contentedly kick my old heels in the air
And enter his mountain before you can say
"Pied Piper of Hamelin, I-o-way."

JACKSON TEAGARDEN *(d. 1964)*

Basin Street is a street
Where dark and light...always meet,
Where I can lose
My Basin Street Blues...

End chorus. Jackson stops singing and slips
the shiny brass dragon trombone to his lips.
Its mouth pours lava from the fire
at the core of the heart where the volcanoes are.
And after the heat has scorched and stung
it licks its wounds with a coiled brass tongue.

This is his personal jubilee:
Sorrow will be the life of me.

Forget all about that silver linin'
that side of the street where the sun keeps shinin'
where the red red robin keeps bob-bob-bobbin'
and nobody's pain is throb-throb-throbbin'.

His was a horn without illusion
blowing an audible crucible fusion
of seven-you-win, ninety-three-you-lose.
He never lost his Basin Street Blues,
nor his exclusive jubilee:
Sorrow will be the life of me.

BILLIE HOLIDAY *(d. 1959)*

She was known as Lady.
In the trade, we all called her Lady,
out of deference, out of acknowledgement, out of love
for her high-brown beauty,
for her high-brown singing.

Did you never hear her
in Harlem hideaways (where the haze of smoke hung heavy)
in joints on 52nd Street (where the competition was cab-horn)
in Hollywood Bowl (where she out-snooted its pretentiousness)?

All right, then.
You will have to settle for phonograph records,
and never see her
wear a dress as green as absinthe, in color and implication,
with lipstick and fingernail polish to match,
looking, though she was not,
proud to insolence
of the lazy, tireless mastery of her throat
over her, over you.

In you a tear lies sleeping,
ready to waken,
and it does,
to the little snake-tongues of her variousness,
darting now out of honey...now out of brine...
out of ginger...hot tar...pistachio...gall.

A SWITCH IN SUBJECT MATTER

Students, today's lesson is jazz music
Try to use your meticulous skill
as draftsmen   if you will   to blueprint
the throw-away joy of a jazzman
in his riff   in his blood-beat rhythm
Today your drawingboard sketches
will calculate no seeming-permanent
highrise in steel and cement
But they may catch the lifebrief   beautyflash
vouchsafed us in flowers and fish

IV. GROWING TIME

FEED ME

Feed me time to be lonely
hermit hours that fortify
I starve on heaped-up commodity
waste away on platters of crowd

Gorge me on isolation
days on end   a strict ration
of womb-stillness, mole-darkness,
earth-heaviness, nourishes

my root-marrow   solitary
I hunger my way to satiety

WINTER PASSES

When all the icicles of hate have thawed;
when ice-bound fists have melted, hoary hearts
and hailstone eyes dissolved in the torrents of Spring;
when we discern that all our arctic smarts
of Winter are an inner seasoning
that may be Summer-solsticed for our need;
then we shall study war no more, shall store
no more the polar armor of despair,
the stock-piled zero terror, forged by fear
in smithies of frozen fire. Then we shall hear
(full-sapped with joy and sluiced with love again)
bombardment of apple blossom, explosion painless
of bud into flower, spurting a hyacinth stain
under the innocent artillery of the rain.

SPARROW   GRASS AND FIELD LILY

Are ye not much better than these?
—Matthew 6:20

Sparrows don't require very
High flying, can be merry
Anywhere, also wary
The way skeptics often are,
And brave, although their valor
Threatens no "Sparrow Power"!
And may be observed only
By an eye as sharp as their own.

Grass could be sparrow's twin:
Identical the spirit
To survive, grin and bear it,
To be earth's gay, green cocked-hat
Things keep getting knocked into,
Yanked out again somehow.
Step on grass, it springs back hale,
Thumbs its nose at your heel,
Covers war's deepest shell hole.

Also consider field lilies
Born such natural beauties
They can ignore all cut-throat
Competition for best-dressed,
Are permanently pressed,
Find drip-dry old-hat,
Innocently unaware
Of any *haute couture,*
Model lush satin and velvet
Divinely cut and fitted.

Against this gentle trinity
Set man: death-duster, bulldozer,
Sky, land, and water defiler—
Still better than these three?

LAKE NIGHTMARE

Nobody dares look in the dark lake
that drowns his pain. Safer to make
manifest diagnosis: headache
tension   allergy   What drug to take?

Simpler to let dark lakes now and then explode
in violent geysers at home or abroad,
the former known as riots, the latter,
wars. Nobody sees them breed.

In the dark lake where nobody dares look
witch-words bubble, reeking of hemlock:
PIG   WASP   RED   BLACK
Hate the unknown unalike.

Easier sailing upon the pleasant surface
closed eyes fixed on the obvious placid
no Lock Nesses topside or outside
all ogres tied up in children's stories.

And so to bed…up from Lake Nightmare then
rises before your terrified eyes the monster:
yourself. Face and fight him if you can,
but, win or lose, tackle the right enemy.

POVERTY PROGRAM

If you get only one reaction
from the sight of a naked body
you're poverty-stricken

If you know only one expression
for truth: *Tell it like it is*
you're indigent

If you have only one solution
to offer dissenters: *Let 'em eat jail*
you're broke

If your exclusive idea of education
for rebels is teach them a lesson:
Hurt them! Shoot them!
you are a pauper

You may, of course, enroll in the program
but I doubt very much that we can help you

TO THE TECHNOLOGIANS: A PETITION

A little more mystery, gentlemen,
a little more awe and wonder
a little less certainty, if you please,
a few fewer graphs and charts,
if you don't mind, penned to control
astonishments to your will
a little less harnessing
of the unknown to your purposes,
searching out the inscrutable
a touch more humility maybe...?

spare the possibly revelatory
prattle of children, of schizics
your vision-destroying techniques
(when enigma speaks, are you listening?)

release the dream from your clinical REM:
know-how, some funnyman said
(can you program humor? wisdom?)
is not the same thing as know-why

suffer the singing bird   comfrey   cricket
to live: forbear wiring the playful dolphin
to heel to your (sometime lethal?) command

LULLABY

Sleep, small dolphin;
Sleep, small snail.
Sleep on silver sea for pillow,
Or leaf of willow.
Now swoop no wing from flowering mallow,
Leap no billow.
Stealthily each wave after its fellow
Slips. Each swallow
Naps. Small dolphin,
Sleep. Small snail,
Sleep, too. Dream home of pearl, and sail,
On leaf of willow and sea for pillow,
Frequently frail.

LOVE SONG

If I were blind, I should not see your eyes,
Now children's bonfires, flickering with delight;
Now hearthfires, warm blue flame through chill blue night;
Now embered in thought, slow-burning, glowing, wise.
I should not see—if I were blind—your hair,
Flaunting its cowlick cockade of youth at the crown
Where cautious age tries vainly to slick it down;
Of all visible wonder of you—were I blind—unaware.
But love has more than one means to an end.
This garden wall, warm to my touch where the sun has climbed,
This lilac-laden, rain-rinsed April air,
That mockingbird lilt of mischievous scorn: this blend
Of things clearer on heart than ever on iris limned
Would summon me still. I should know that you were there.

THE SOUND GOD MAKES

Touch me anywhere at all,
Head, hip, shoulder, shin,
I ring like a bell, quiver like a crystal,
Give off the god-tone.

Here is the perfect A of the oboe
To which all the instruments tune,
Orchestrating the perfect echo
Of the sound God makes. Listen…!

Stay as close to the Source as you can.
Let the music expand within you
Until like an over-full fountain
You spill over with the sound of God.

SOLSTICE

Year's at winter solstice. Me, too.
Bare-branched in spirit. Root-dry.
Knowing it's time to display
the ancient life-stir promise,

the older-than-Odin evergreen
hung with bright bauble and star-shine,
time to Trim the Tree, the sign of
the Coming, aborning, hidden,

in soil or in Bethlehem—
but not in my living room.
I lift my leaden head. Pure random.
Outside, under the street light's star-blue dome,

magnolia leaves glitter, wet
with winter rain, gem-faceted
by winter's cutting wind. What
Tree was ever so scintillate?

How dare I deaden? Winter
herself wombs the dormant life-stir.
Solsticed together, she has showed me
all the shining Tree promise I need.

GROWTH

This seed was buried deeper
in soil richer
than any I have cultivated before.
The new shoots have a more delicate texture;
buds whisper
open to a darker flower
than any I am accustomed (their fragrance is subtler)
to live with.

Even the fledglings that flutter
to this plant are rarer:
that garnet-crested one, for instance, has never
appeared before; his song at this twilight hour
stirs me more urgently than ever
I heard bird at dawn. Also, the flowers
now glow like embers
banked against the Sabbath
of all agriculture.

I grow towards my death.

MAN — PLANT

My new-grown man is raining home
at last. Rest and harvest him.

Bedded, seeded, tamped down,
blacked out, wormed in,

buried. Such a sad-begot!
Walk away…let rot

That's the way I thought it was.
But life-stubborn Earth pays

very scant attention to
our appraisal of her value.

She brings forth in season—hers,
never death-stubborn ours.

Drenched in benefit, I raise a jorum
of sweat and rain to her wisdom:

she bids me reap (she knows our need)
a crop I never knew I sowed.

THE WINTER EYE

Sees no locust swarm of flower
Gardens are gone to pod and seed
Spume of color and fragrance fled
Buxom Summer denuded
Squadrons of insects flown from the meadows
Brook sparkle blotted out by ice
The reaches of the beaches bare
Of umbrellas   transistors   girls in bikinis
Seagulls filling the space with grace...

Less of clutter, more of matter
Less to see, more to contemplate:
A scrawl of twig on a blank sheet of snow
One red berry dotting an *i*
Which hasn't changed since Xerxes was...
In landscape stripped to survival size
The winter eye keener focuses
To find something worth looking at

COVENANT

My father's face lit up the living room,
the sun having set, the lights not yet turned on,
the fiddle tucked under his chin, his knees spread
in the orchestra-pit position he remembered
from his days as "Mr. Leader" in a vaudeville house
(four shows a day, five on weekends and holidays)
"I could still do it, play in some restaurant or dance hall,"
he said. And the weather in that room turned covenantal,
the bright rainbow of his face a token of promise,
shimmeringly set on the cloud of my tears
since I knew that for him to play again was impossible.
Damaged nerves now sent the hand confused signals
(his hand was beautiful; my own was gened
to that look: squat, big-knuckled, a working hand)
Where was that middle? This string...that finger...
But it came out all wrong, all the sounds a-jangle,
fingers out of control on the familiar strings,
the notes grasped-for always just out of reach,
mocking the bright bow that promised so much.

When he died, my mother said it was a pity
he never was able to play it the way he wanted
(his vibrato, for instance, always was uneven)
never could make it sound the way he heard it
(where? in his "bum" ear? The Orphan's Home neglected it)
I never could make her see how little it mattered
that, as the jargon goes, he never "made it,"
never succeeded in getting what he wanted,
nor expected to find it waiting for him in Heaven.

For sixty years he worked hard. He loved my mother,
told jokes and the truth, one spontaneous as the other;
he let the promise do what the doing lacked,
seagulling free of the tricky shoals of fact,
staying Springful of budding in any old Winter.
His playing needed no instrument—the Innocent!
The means of his living rendered the end unimportant.

CRADLE SONG

His voice was faint in Bethlehem
    As new-born babies' voices are;
And yet it arrowed across the sand
    To fetch the doughty Balthazar.

So weak the voice in Bethlehem
    It scarcely reached the stable door;
Yet from a distant Eastern land
    It drew the dauntless Melchior.

A baby's voice in Bethlehem,
    More than most babies', indiscreet;
(Hush....Herod...!) yet Kaspar, from Samarkand,
    Sped to the tiny, dangerous feet.

The voice that wakened in Bethlehem,
    Slept nevermore, in stall or bier.
Ho! Brother Wise Men, do we still stand
    And listen with lion-hearted ear?

WEEDS

My little purslane, henbit, knawel,
the oddity of love is all
you need to know.
Weeds grow
and tendril our idiot hearts as well
as orchid, rose, or asphodel.

You short, bald, and homely turtle-
dove…or lank-haired, horn-rimmed jewel,
never ask why
some she or he
adores you: love is not love that's rational
not mc^2, but Tinkerbell.

The book you dote on is clearly awful;
ever decently critical
reviewer says so.
What's that to you—
aware that the Garden of Love is full
of riffraff horticultural
daftly, privately lovable.

GROWING TIME

Seeding is a method:
the wind can seed
or a bird   or scattering coattail
a machine   or a male

Now comes growing time…

How is it with the rhizome
    cocoon   pippin
    foetus   spawn
    kernel   pod
moistly   pregnantly   buried
in the shrouded gestating tomb
of ground   stream   shell   womb

    22 months till an elephant
     6   till baboon
     9   till child

across the alfalfa field
the Spring-green stitching

new life emerging
after the hidden brooding
in the dark of below   within

the wonder pondered by Mary
bearing the answer
the no man's land
women understand

TRAVELER

happy to be lost at last
past map   compass   signal fire
quit of the baggage of mistrust
marking the unruly traveler

who never wants to go where the tour
directs   finds its ports of call
drab   its slide rule itinerary
grubby   touted fetes dull

finally errantly landed here
alight in this uncharted place
transported by the everywhere
rare air of nowhereness

GOLD OF A CERTAIN KIND

"...the sound of his language is the essence and soul of his
meaning. Sunt lacrimæ rerum..."
—*Rolfe Humphries*

Sleeper, awake! You are about to make gold.

    Procedure becomes clear
    from the sound of the chosen word:
    the chosen word, say, is ERROR
    (not mistake   fault   blunder)

    Roll the word round in your ear
    it ends as it begins
    turns back on itself
    echoes endlessly

    becomes the essence—
    Listen!—
    of your meaning. No other word
    forms crucible here

    You have chosen ERROR
    because you hear
    that fault   mistake   blunder
    produce no uroboros,

    wondrous tail-eating serpent,
    no *prima materia*
    to initiate the alchemy
    that turns lead into gold.

Sleeper, awake! You are about to make gold.
    That is what the man said.